The Gardener's Journal

With Illustrations and Quotations

RUNNING PRESS
PHILADELPHIA · LONDON

9   8   7   6   5   4   3   2   1
Digit on the right indicates the number of this printing.

ISBN 0-7624-0074-9

Cover and interior illustrations by Christopher Wormell
Cover design by Diane Miljat
Interior design by Corinda Cook
Edited by Gena M. Pearson
Typography: Aperto and Caslon

This book may be ordered by mail from the publisher.
Please include $2.50 for postage and handling.
But try your bookstore first!

Running Press Book Publishers
125 South Twenty-second Street
Philadelphia, Pennsylvania 19103-4399

To Melanie –
With love from Grandma – 2000

The Gardener's Journal

A<small>LL FOR THE LOVE OF FLOWERS.</small>

—Linnaeus
(1707–1778)
Swedish botanist

Flowers are words which even a baby may understand.

—*Arthur C. Coxe (b. 1900)*
English writer

To CREATE A LITTLE FLOWER IS THE LABOR OF AGES.

—*William Blake* (*1757–1827*)
English poet

When you take a flower in your hand and really look at it, it's your world for the moment.

—*Georgia O'Keeffe (1887–1986)*
American painter

The flower that you hold in your hands was born today and already it is as old as you are.

—*Antonio Porchia (1886–1968)*
Italian-born Argentinean writer

The Amen! of Nature is always a flower.

—*Oliver Wendell Holmes Sr. (1809–1894)*
American philosopher

ARE NOT FLOWERS THE STARS OF EARTH AND
ARE NOT OUR STARS THE FLOWERS OF HEAVEN?

—*Anonymous*

THOU CANS'T NOT
STIR A FLOWER WITHOUT
TROUBLING OF A STAR.

—*Francis Thompson*
(1859–1907)
English writer

Flowers changed the face of the planet.
Without them, the world we know—
even man himself—would never have existed.

—*Loren Eiseley (1907–1977)*
American anthropologist

Each flower is a
soul opening out
to nature.

—*Gerard de Nerval*
(1808–1855)
French writer

F LOWERS. THEY ARE THE CELEBRATION
OF THE CHANGING OF THE SEASONS
AND THE CONFIRMATION THAT
NATURAL BEAUTY IS EVERYWHERE.

—*Jo Packham*
American writer

W hat can better define beauty than a flower?

—*Paul Goodnight (b. 1946)*
American artist

A FLOWER IS THE MOST ELIGIBLE OBJECT IN THE WORLD.

—*Donita A. Ferguson*
American gardener

LIKE JEWELS, THE FLOWERING ANNUALS HAVE ONE PRIMARY PURPOSE:
TO DELIGHT THE EYE. AND LIKE JEWELS, THEY DELIGHT IN MANY WAYS,
FORMALLY OR INFORMALLY, SETTING OFF BACKGROUND, COLORS FRAMING
FEATURES, CALLING ATTENTION TO FOCAL POINTS. BUT THEY CAN ALSO
SURPASS JEWELS, FOR AS LIVING FLOWERS THEY APPEAL TO ALL THE SENSES.
THE SILKEN SHELLS OF PETUNIAS OR THE VELVETY PETALS OF SALPIGLOSSIS
ALMOST ASK TO BE TOUCHED. THE PUNGENCY OF MARIGOLDS FILLS A WARM
SUMMER DAY; AS THE LIGHT FAILS, EVENING STOCK FRESHENS THE AIR. . . .
AND ONE CAN EVEN HEAR THE WHISPERING SOUNDS OF RABBIT-TAILS
OR QUAKING GRASS WHEN THE BREEZE RUSTLES ITS SLENDER STALKS.

—James Underwood Crockett
American writer

The best-looking flowers are the ones growing untended along the sides of the road, in the fields, or in the woods.

WHEN IT COMES TO BEAUTY, I CAN THINK OF
NOTHING GREATER OR MORE INSPIRING THAN A FIELD
OF BLOOMING MARIGOLDS TOSSING THEIR HEADS IN THE
SUNSHINE AND GIVING A GLOW TO THE ENTIRE LANDSCAPE.

—*Everett McKinley Dirksen* (1869–1969)
U.S. Senator

M arigolds are bright and beautiful, like cousins,
you don't have too many of them at once.

—Henry Mitchell
American writer

IT IS NOW THE SIXTH HOUR; THE SWEET TIME OF THE MORNING; AND THE SUN AT EVERY WINDOW CALLS SLEEPERS FROM THEIR BEDS. THE MARIGOLD BEGINS TO OPEN HER EYES, AND THE DEW ON THE GROUND DOTH SWEETEN THE AIR.

—Nicholas Breton
16th-century English writer

You cannot forget if you would those golden kisses all over the cheeks of the meadow, queerly called dandelions.

—*Henry Ward Beecher (1813–1887)*
American cleric

What was paradise? but a garden,
an orchard of trees and herbs, full of
pleasure, and nothing there but delights.

—*William Lawson (1857–1925)*
American writer

You've seen lilacs wet by rain? Perfect—a mingling
of diamond bracelets and Concord grapes.

—*Allan Gurganus (b. 1947)*
American writer

ONLY THE FLOWER SANCTIFIES THE VASE.

—*Robert Underwood Johnson* (*1853–1937*)
American writer and editor

How can one help shivering with delight when
one's hot fingers close around the stem of a live flower,
cool from the shade and stiff with newborn vigor!

—Colette (1873–1954)
French writer

No flower is really understood
until we have seen it both in the mass
and individually; at a distance and in the hand.

—*Richardson Wright*
American writer

WHEN I TOUCH THAT FLOWER, I AM TOUCHING INFINITY.
IT EXISTED LONG BEFORE THERE WERE HUMAN BEINGS
ON THIS EARTH AND WILL CONTINUE TO EXIST FOR MILLIONS
OF YEARS TO COME. THROUGH THE FLOWER, I TALK TO
THE INFINITE, WHICH IS ONLY A SILENT FORCE. THIS IS NOT
A PHYSICAL CONTACT. IT IS NOT THE EARTHQUAKE, WIND
OR FIRE. IT IS IN THE INVISIBLE WORLD. IT IS THAT STILL SMALL
VOICE THAT CALLS UP THE FAIRIES.

—*George Washington Carver*
(1864–1943)
American botanist

W hen my hoe tinkled against the stones,
that music echoed to the woods and sky,
and was an accompaniment to my labor.

—*Henry David Thoreau (1817–1862)*
American writer

TO ANALYZE THE CHARMS OF FLOWERS IS LIKE DISSECTING MUSIC;
IT IS ONE OF THE THINGS WHICH IT IS FAR BETTER TO ENJOY,
THAN TO ATTEMPT FULLY TO UNDERSTAND.

—*Henry Theodore Tuckerman*
American writer

Flowers . . . have a mysterious
and subtle influence upon the feelings,
not unlike some strains of music.
They relax the tenseness of the mind.
They dissolve its rigor.

—*Henry Ward Beecher*
(1813–1887)
American cleric

We cannot fathom the mystery of a single flower,
nor is it intended that we should. . . .

—*John Ruskin (1819–1900)*
English writer

THE STRANGE THING WHICH I HAVE EXPERIENCED
WITH FLOWER SCENTS, AND INDEED WITH ALL OTHER
SCENTS, IS THAT THEY ONLY RECALL PLEASANT MEMORIES.

—*Theodore A. Stephens* (b. *1907*)
English editor

[A garden] should be a place of sweet scent and sentiment.

—*Alice Lounsberry*
American writer

Deep in their roots,
All flowers keep the light.

—*Theodore Roethke*
(1908–1963)
American poet

PERFECT IN ITS BUD AS IN ITS BLOOM,
WITH NO REASON TO EXPLAIN ITS PRESENCE,
NO MISSION TO FULFILL.

—*James McNeill Whistler* (1834–1903)
American painter

Ever since I could remember anything, flowers
have been like dear friends to me—comforters,
inspirers, powers to uplift and to cheer.

—*Celia Thaxter (1835–1894)*
American writer

Gardens . . . are familiar friends.

—*Thalassa Cruso*
English-born American
gardener and journalist

I'D LIKE TO INTRODUCE
YOU TO SOME FRIENDS
OF MINE—THE FLOWERS.

—Denise Diamond
American lecturer

People from a planet without flowers would think we must be mad with joy the whole time to have such things about us.

—*Iris Murdoch (b. 1919)*
Irish-born English novelist

WHATEVER A MAN'S AGE, HE CAN REDUCE IT SEVERAL YEARS
BY PUTTING A BRIGHT-COLORED FLOWER IN HIS BUTTONHOLE.

—*Mark Twain* (1835–1910)
American writer

I recommend that all bachelors have a garden.
It will give them, in some small way,
the experience of being a parent.

—Richard Goodman
American writer

"JUST LIVING IS NOT ENOUGH," SAID THE BUTTERFLY.
"ONE MUST HAVE SUNSHINE, FREEDOM, AND A LITTLE FLOWER."

—*Hans Christian Andersen* (1805–1875)
Danish writer

Earth laughs in flowers.

—*Ralph Waldo Emerson (1803–1882)*
American writer

THERE'S ROSEMARY, THAT'S FOR REMEMBRANCE:
PRAY, YOU, LOVE, REMEMBER: AND THERE IS
PANSIES, THAT'S FOR THOUGHTS. . . .

—*William Shakespeare* (1564–1616)
English dramatist and poet

Rare flower, leaf fringed, of tender yellow-gold—
what could prevent a beautiful girl from
     casually smelling it?
I almost thought it was her lover's mouth
     imprinted in the center.

—*Chang Yu*
9th-century Chinese poet

To SEE A WORLD IN A GRAIN OF SAND
AND A HEAVEN IN A WILD FLOWER.

—*William Blake* (1757–1827)
English poet

If you like flowers, give them.

If you love flowers, grow them.

—*Jo Packham*
American writer

Find out what you can grow and grow lots of it.

—*Lord Lascelles Abercrombie*
19th-century English horticulturist

Love of flowers and all things green
and growing is with many men and women
a passion so strong that it often seems to
be a sort of primal instinct, coming down
through generation after generation, from
the first man who was put into a garden
"to dress it and to keep it."

—Helena Rutherford Ely
American writer

GARDENING IS THE BEST THERAPY IN THE WORLD.

YOU CAN PUT SO MUCH INTO IT AN GET SO MUCH BACK.

—*C. Z. Guest*
American journalist

Gardening ministers to the needs of the soul which sometimes hungers, thirsts and shivers, while the body is luxuriously fed and clothed in fine raiment.

—*Frank M. Lupton*
19th-century American farmer

S OIL WARMS OUR HANDS AND OUR SOULS AS WE WORK IN IT.

—*Allen Lacy* (*b. 1935*)
American writer

Flowers are to nourish the soul,
the bread to nourish the body.

—*Hal Cook*
American flower arranger

Buy hyacinths to feed thy soul.

—*Sadi*
13th-century Persian poet

THE EARTH NEEDED NOURISHMENT AND CARE . . .
I NEEDED NOURISHMENT AND CARE MYSELF.
WHAT BETTER SOURCE THAN MY GARDEN?

—*Janice Emily Bowers*
American botanist

FLOWERS AND PLANTS ARE SILENT PRESENCES:
THEY NOURISH EVERY SENSE EXCEPT THE EAR.

—May Sarton (1912–1995)
American writer and poet

The greatest gift of a garden is
the restoration of the five senses.

—Hanna Rion
19th-centrury American writer

THE GARDEN IS THE PLACE I GO TO FOR REFUGE AND SHELTER, NOT THE HOUSE. . . .

—*Elizabeth von Arnim* (*1866–1941*)
English writer

Home is where the garden grows.

—George Shenk
American gardener and writer

But gardens are places in which men come home again. . . .

—*Terry Comito (b. 1935)*
English historian

To ME A GARDEN IS AN AREA, OR A SERIES OF RELATED AREAS,
WHEREIN ONE FINDS REASSURANCE AND TRANQUILLITY, SURPRISE
AND DELIGHT. . . . SUCH A GARDEN IMPARTS A BENEDICTION,
ENLARGING THE MENTAL AND EMOTIONAL HABITATION. . . .

—Josephine Nueues
American writer

B**Y A GARDEN IS MEANT MYSTICALLY
A PLACE OF SPIRITUAL REPOSE. STILL-
NESS. PEACE. REFRESHMENT. DELIGHT.**

—*John Henry Newman*
(1801–1890)
English theologian and writer

[I am] never happier than when I am on my hands and knees,
dressed in baggy clothes, caked with dirt, a baseball hat
cocked on my head to shield the sun, my dogs at my side,
the telephone out of reach, weeding my flower beds.

—Page Dickey
American writer and illustrator

I KNOW A LITTLE GARDEN CLOSE,
SET THICK WITH LILY AND RED ROSES,
WHERE I WOULD WANDER IF I MIGHT
FROM DEWY MORN TO DEWY NIGHT.

—William Morris (1834–1896)
English poet

A LITTLE GARDEN IN WHICH TO WALK,
AN IMMENSITY IN WHICH TO DREAM.

—*Victor Hugo* (1802–1885)
French writer

All my hurts
My garden spade can heal. A woodland walk,
A quest of river-grapes, a mocking thrush,
A wild-rose, or rock-loving columbine.
Salve my worst wounds.

—*Ralph Waldo Emerson (1803–1882)*
American writer and philosopher

Love your garden, and work in it, and let it give you what it surely
will of sweetness [and] health . . . and let no one feel that the benefit is all
on the side of the garden, for truly you will receive more than you give.

—*Louise B. Wilder* (1879–1938)
American writer

The more one gardens, the more one learns; and the more one learns, the more one realizes how little one knows. I suppose the whole of life is like that: the endless fight against one thing or another, whether it be green-flies on the roses or the complexity of personal relationships.

—Victoria Sackville-West (1892–1962)
English writer

Gardens are intended for meditation. . . .

—*Dorothy Graham (1893–1959)*
American writer

YOUR GARDEN WILL REVEAL YOURSELF.

—*Henry Mitchell*
American gardener

As is the gardener, so is the garden.

—*Thomas Fuller (1608–1661)*
English writer

Few GARDENS HAVE THE GRANDEUR OF CATHEDRALS. OFTEN SMALL, THEY
ARE CREATIONS OF THEIR OWNER—EXPRESSIONS OF FAITH AND CONVICTION.

—*Elsa Bakalar*
English-born American writer

Something happens when I dig, especially if the soil is soft and my shovel is sharp. Digging by hand, I get to know my garden from end to end and side to side.

—Janice Emily Bowers
American botanist

Working with the soil doesn't automatically endow a man with either wisdom or philosophy, but it does make him aware of orderly sequences such as night and day, summer and winter, bud, blossom, and seed. And of such certainties as life, death, and change. Knowing those things, a man can live with himself and probably get along with his neighbors.

—*Hal Borland (1900–1978)*
American writer

ALL GARDENS HAVE SOMETHING
TO YIELD IN THE WAY OF WISDOM.

—*Margaret Elphinstone*
American gardener

A fine garden is a beautiful thing, and the person who tills, plants, and cultivates it has every reason to be proud. But the ultimate success is when the gardener also grows.

—*Virgil Adams*
American columnist

M Y GARDEN LIKE MY LIFE,
SEEMS TO ME EVERY YEAR TO WANT
CORRECTION AND REQUIRE ALTERATION.

—Alexander Pope (1688–1744)
English poet

GARDENING OFFERS A CHANCE FOR MAN

TO REGULATE AT LEAST ONE ASPECT OF HIS LIFE,

TO CONTROL HIS ENVIRONMENT. . . .

—*Ann Leighton*
American gardener

Gardening is like cooking: read the recipe
and then use your head. A dash of skepticism
can do no harm. Go lightly on caution,
heavily on adventure, and see what comes out.
If you make a mistake, what of it? That is
one way to learn, and tomorrow is another day.

—*Ruth Stout*
American gardener

A MAN'S MIND MAY BE LIKENED TO A GARDEN,
WHICH MAY BE INTELLIGENTLY CULTIVATED OR
ALLOWED TO RUN WILD; BUT WHETHER CULTIVATED
OR NEGLECTED, IT MUST, AND WILL BRING FORTH.

—*James Allen (b. 1929)*
American writer

HE WAS NO LOVER OF GARDEN FLOWERS ONLY:
THE WILD AND THE WEEDS EVEN HAD ALWAYS A FASCINATION FOR HIM.

—*Virginia Woolf* (1882–1941)
English writer

What is a weed?
A plant whose virtues
have not yet been discovered.

—*Ralph Waldo Emerson*
(1803–1882)
American essayist and poet

At the moment of planting a bulb,
all is hope, no dismay. Then there
is surely something hauntingly symbolic
about burying a living thing toward
a sure resurrection, at a moment in the
season when everything else is dying
or on the way out.

—*May Sarton (1912–1995)*
American writer

He who plants a garden,
plants happiness.

—*Chinese proverb*

THE GREATEST SERVICE WHICH CAN BE RENDERED
ANY COUNTRY IS TO ADD A USEFUL PLANT TO ITS CULTURE.

—*Thomas Jefferson* (1743–1826)
American president

Gardening is not a recipe you follow,
it's a relationship you live.

—*Pat Stone*
American gardener

AND THE GLORY OF THE GARDEN SHALL NEVER PASS AWAY.

—Rudyard Kipling (1865–1936)
English writer

When we see the garden
as a blend of art and science,
history and dreams, it can
be an unencumbered source
of wonder and joy.

—*Jennifer Bennett*
Canadian writer

No occupation is so delightful to me as the culture of the earth, and no culture comparable to that of the garden.

—*Thomas Jefferson* (1743–1826)
American president

The garden was a celebration, a destination.

—Anne Rivers Siddons (b. 1936)
American writer

No joy is so great in life of seclusion as that of gardening. No matter what the soil may be, sandy or heavy clay, on a hill or a slope, it will serve well.

—*Walafrid Strabo, Abbot of Reichenau*
9th-century Swiss writer

To own a bit of ground, to scratch it with a hoe, to plant seeds, and watch the renewal of life—this is the commonest delight of the race, the most satisfactory thing a man can do.

—Charles Dudley Warner (1829–1900)
American editor and writer

I love to wander around
my garden and sniff the sneezewort,
tweak the old man, wince at
the birthwort or perhaps wonder
if I should pick a bunch of fleabane
and hang it over the cat's basket.

—*Penny Black*
English horticultural
artist and writer

TENDING THE GREEN THINGS THAT GROW
KEEPS THE GARDENER IN TOUCH WITH
THE UNLABORED WAY THAT NATURE GOVERNS.

—Joan Lee Faust
American writer

WE MAY NOT BE ABLE TO MAINTAIN OUR EARLY FANTASIES OF GARDEN MAKING.
WE MAY HAVE TO GIVE UP ON A TWO-HUNDRED-FOOT-LONG PERENNIAL BORDER. . . .
BUT THERE WILL BE OTHER ILLUSIONS TO REPLACE THEM. . . .THERE WILL ALSO BE
DELIGHTS WE COULD HARDLY HAVE IMAGINED. BUT ONLY IF WE KEEP ON GARDENING.

—Patricia Thorpe
American writer

What nature delivers to us is never stale.
Because what nature creates has eternity in it.

—*Isaac Bashevis Singer (b. 1904)*
Polish-born American writer

Roses become compost;
compost feeds the garden
for the growth of new roses.

—*Buddha [Siddhartha Guatama]*
(563 B.C.–483 B.C.)
Indian philosopher

GARDENING IS IN ITS PERFECT STATE,
A TRUE GIVE-AND-TAKE RELATIONSHIP.

—Richard Goodman
American writer

^Old gardens have
a language of their own. . . .

—Gertrude Huntington McGiffert
American poet

Meeting new persons, entertaining new ideas, viewing new scenes, lend zest and freshness to life. The gardener finds this same zest in making the acquaintance of plants that are new to him.

—*Louise Beebe Wilder*
(1878–1938)
American writer

PLANTING A SEED IS AN ACT OF FAITH.

—*Barbara Kingsolver* (b. 1955)
American writer

CONVINCE ME THAT YOU HAVE A SEED THERE,
AND I AM PREPARED TO EXPECT WONDERS.

—*Henry David Thoreau* (1817–1862)
American writer

THE SICKLY ORCHID

    THAT I TENDED SO . . .

    AT LAST

THANKS ME WITH A BUD.

      —Taigo [Wangsa] (1301–1382)
      Korean monk

About the Illustrator

Christopher Wormell is the author and illustrator of the best-selling children's book, *An Alphabet of Animals*, winner of the Graphics Prize at the Bologna Book Fair in 1990. A self-taught artist who dropped out of school at age 18 to pursue painting, he began engraving in 1982 and has won worldwide recognition as an illustrator. An *Alphabet of Animals* was followed by an illustrated edition of *Mowgli's Brothers*, the first story of Rudyard Kipling's *The Jungle Book*, and *A Number of Animals*, which was featured on The New York Times list of books of the year.